The smallest scorpion lives in South America.

Scorpions are *venomous*, which means their sting injects a poison that kills its victims. However, a scorpion sting is often no more harmful to humans than a bee sting.

There are more than 1,500 different kinds of scorpions around the world, from the deserts of the U.S.A. to the mountains of Asia. Most are 2 to 3 inches long. The largest American species is the desert hairy scorpion. The world's largest is the African scorpion, at over 8 inches!

Desert Hairy Scorpion

North America's largest species is the 6-inch desert hairy scorpion. This giant lives in the deserts of the American Southwest. Like all scorpions, it has poor eyesight. It "sees" by sensing vibrations in the air and ground. During the day, it sleeps in the shade of rocks—but come nightfall, it creeps out to hunt other scorpions, lizards, and small snakes.

SCORPIONS
SPIDERS, CENTIPEDES AND MILLIPEDES

LEVEL 3 READER

READING LEVEL 3 GRADES 2 TO 4

Written by Paul Kupperberg

The CREATIVE EDGE name is a trademark of Dalmatian Publishing Group,
Franklin, Tennessee 37068-2068. 1-800-815-8696.

CreativeEdge2340110056F16842264-03/10

Scorpions

Scorpions have existed since prehistoric times. They are *arachnids*—eight-legged creatures that belong to the same family as spiders, mites, and ticks. Their big pincers (claws) give them a crab- or lobster-like appearance. See that long tail? It's topped with a stinger!

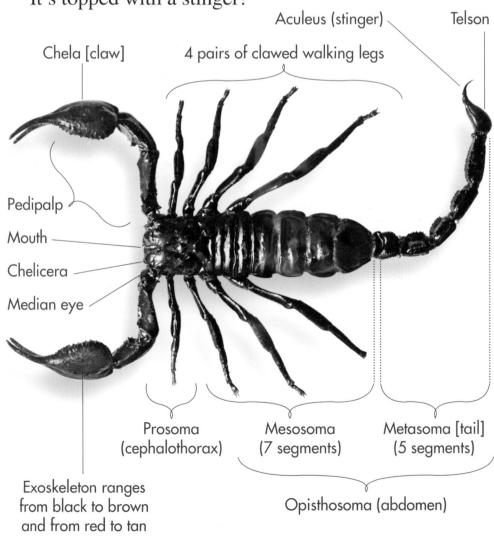

Aculeus (stinger)

Telson

Chela [claw]

4 pairs of clawed walking legs

Pedipalp

Mouth

Chelicera

Median eye

Prosoma (cephalothorax)

Mesosoma (7 segments)

Metasoma [tail] (5 segments)

Exoskeleton ranges from black to brown and from red to tan

Opisthosoma (abdomen)

Sand Scorpion

Sand scorpions also live in the American desert. Their pale color helps them blend in with the sand. Their legs have bristly combs which help them crawl easily over the sand in their night-time hunt for food. They sense vibrations that travel through the sand—then jab prey with their stinger. Spiders and large insects are their favorite midnight snacks.

Stripe-Tailed Scorpion

If you're camping out beneath the stars in Arizona or New Mexico, be sure to check under your sleeping bag before you crawl in. You may have a visitor! The stripe-tailed scorpion, also known as the devil scorpion, likes to burrow under flat surfaces for protection.

Indian Red Scorpion

The Indian red scorpion is one of the smallest scorpions—but also one of the deadliest! It may be beautiful, but its venom can kill a human. It uses its huge pincers to hold its prey while its stinger delivers the venom. This tiny creature lives in the dry desert areas of India and feeds on insects, spiders, centipedes, and other scorpions.

Emperor Scorpion

The emperor scorpion has been around for 300 million years! These giants of the scorpion kingdom, found in West Africa and the Ivory Coast, grow to 8 inches long and can weigh more than 2 ounces. They are usually shiny black with reddish pincers and stingers. They dig tunnels in the soil of rainforests and under rocks and logs. Unlike most scorpions, the emperor hunts during the day, feeding on insects and other scorpions.

Actual size!

Emperor scorpions are less aggressive than other scorpions, and their venom is mild. For this reason, the emperor is sometimes kept as a pet! Would you want one? They may be quiet and clean—and they do live for 6 to 8 years—but think how hard it would be to find a pet sitter while you're on vacation! Plus, it's best to let them be in the wild. Over-hunting has made this handsome scorpion a threatened species.

Spiders

Spiders are amazing creatures. There are 40,000 different kinds and you'll find them everywhere on Earth, except Antarctica. Like scorpions, these arachnids have eight legs. Instead of stingers, spiders have fangs for injecting poison and *enzymes* into their prey. The enzymes are chemicals that liquefy the spider's victim. It's much easier for a spider to slurp than chew. Spiders also have special organs called spinnerets that produce strands of silk.

The silk is extremely strong and sticky—perfect for building webs and wrapping around prey.

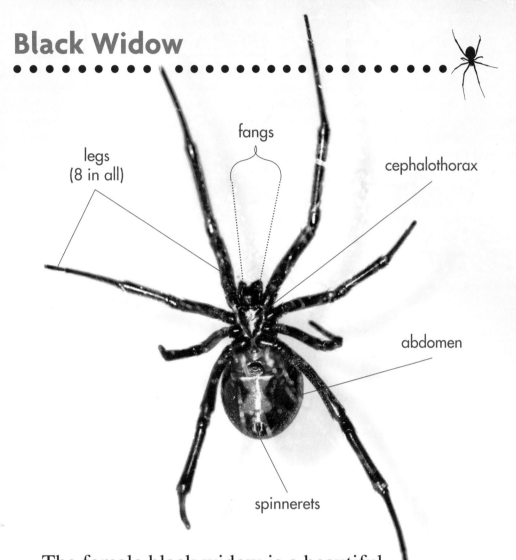

legs
(8 in all)

fangs

cephalothorax

abdomen

spinnerets

The female black widow is a beautiful, shiny black or brown with a red hourglass-shaped mark on her abdomen. The male is much smaller and rarely seen. Do you know why? Because the female often kills and eats the male—making her a widow, indeed. The female black widow is the most poisonous spider in North America, so it's best to stay clear of this lady.

American House Spider

That large web in the dark corner of your room is probably the work of the American house spider. These are fairly friendly houseguests, ranging in color from dirty white to almost black. Left undisturbed, they go about their business of spinning sticky webs to trap flies, mosquitoes, and small moths. The house spider may move from corner to corner until it finds just the right spot for a well-visited web site.

Jumping Spider

Those eyes really jump out at you! Like most spiders, jumping spiders have four pairs of eyes. Their eyes can see in several directions at once, so spiders are good at spotting prey. Jumping spiders are common in the U.S. These brightly colored little creatures can jump 10 to 40 times the length of their own bodies—and they're fast, too!

Daddy-Longlegs

The daddy-longlegs, or harvestman, is not actually a spider. It *is* an arachnid, but it is more closely related to ticks and mites and has been around a long, long time. Some fossilized harvestmen have been found that are 400-million years old! Unlike spiders, daddy-longlegs do not weave webs or inject enzymes that liquefy their prey. Instead, they eat solid food, including small insects and plants.

Wolf Spider

The wolf spider is a large wanderer found almost everywhere, from woodlands to your backyard. They are excellent hunters who either chase their prey or lie in wait to pounce on passing insects. The female wolf spider is a protective mother. She carries her eggs with her in a round globe of webbing stuck to her stomach.

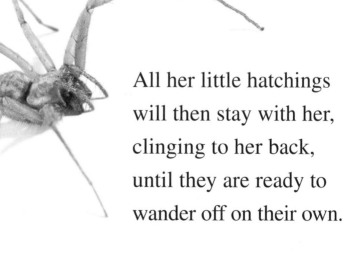

All her little hatchings will then stay with her, clinging to her back, until they are ready to wander off on their own.

Garden Spider

Garden spiders are some of the most attractive spiders in the world. Many have beautiful yellow or orange markings, and their large webs feature fascinating designs. Garden spider webs are large, often 2 feet wide, spun between plants or in windows and doorways. This busy spider will eat its prey and then rebuild part of its web each morning to keep it tidy and "clump-free."

Tarantula

Watch out! Is this a big, hairy monster? No! It's a tarantula, a large spider of the tropics and desert regions. Its venom is weaker than a bee's sting and harmless to humans. These giants are ambush hunters. They eat mainly insects, but the largest tarantulas will hunt frogs, mice, and small birds. Some live in silk-lined burrows. Others live in trees. A tarantula will shed its *exoskeleton* (hard outer covering) several times in its life, and can even re-grow its stomach lining or lost legs.

Centipedes

In Latin, *centi* means *hundred* and *ped* means *foot*. Despite their name, most centipedes have fewer than 100 feet, although some do have more than 300. Centipedes are not arachnids or insects. They are *chilopods*. Every centipede has an odd number of body segments, each with a pair of legs. They have a set of *forcipules* (venom claws) that hold onto prey and inject poison. Many centipedes are no more than an inch long. The largest, the Amazonian giant centipede, is about 12 inches (30 cm) long and can catch a bat out of the air.

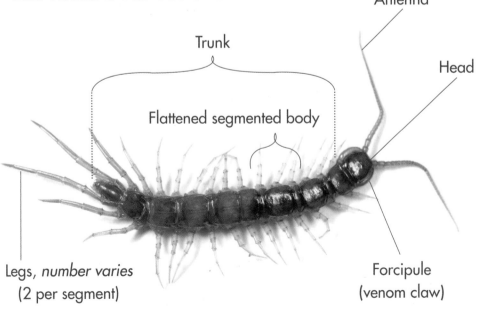

Antenna

Head

Trunk

Flattened segmented body

Legs, *number varies* (2 per segment)

Forcipule (venom claw)

Garden centipedes are found all over North America and Europe. They are between 2 and 3 inches long and have 40 to 80 pairs of short legs. They live in soil and leaf litter, coming out at night to hunt insects and spiders. When you turn over a large rock in your garden, you may see one of these fellows wiggling away. For this reason, they are also called the snake centipede.

House Centipede

Have you ever turned on a basement light and seen a slithery, feathery critter flit across the wall or floor? That was probably a house centipede, which is common in many parts of the world. These yellow-gray hunters feed on spiders and insects. They have 15 pairs of long, delicate legs that are strong and quick. House centipedes can race along surfaces at speeds of up to *16 feet per second!*

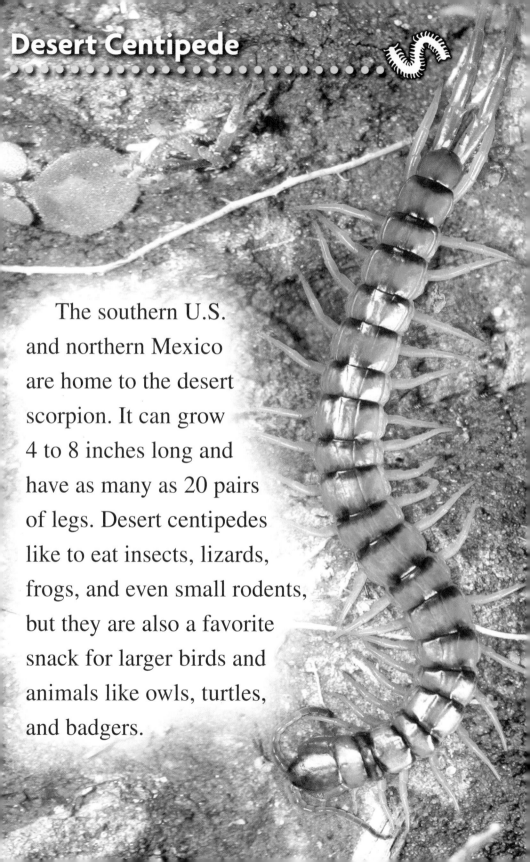

Desert Centipede

The southern U.S. and northern Mexico are home to the desert scorpion. It can grow 4 to 8 inches long and have as many as 20 pairs of legs. Desert centipedes like to eat insects, lizards, frogs, and even small rodents, but they are also a favorite snack for larger birds and animals like owls, turtles, and badgers.

Millipedes

Millipede means *thousand-footed*, but most millipedes have only 36 to 400 legs, although one species can have as many as 750. Millipedes may look like centipedes, but they are *diplopods*. Unlike centipedes, millipedes are slow moving and harmless, living on decaying leaves and plants. They can, however, cause damage to gardens when they choose to munch on seedlings. Most millipedes are 1 to 4 inches long. The 11-inch African centipede is often kept as a pet.

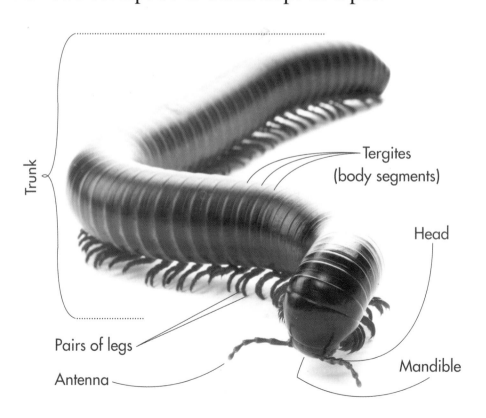

Trunk

Tergites
(body segments)

Head

Pairs of legs

Antenna

Mandible

North American Millipede

North American millipedes like living where it is dark and moist, such as fields and forests. They can grow to 3 inches long. They creep along very slowly, but will quickly curl up into a tight coil if disturbed. Millipedes can also release a disgusting smell that makes them less than tasty to attackers.

Flat Millipede

Most millipedes are cylindrical, having a rounded, tube-like shape. The flat millipede, however, has a flattened body form. Some have striking yellow markings, warning predators to steer clear of the foul smell and taste. Flat millipedes live under rocks or logs and feed on decaying plants. Sometimes for a special treat, they will snack on strawberries and other fruit. Even creepy crawlies have a sweet side!